Interesting Correspondence.

LETTER

OF

COMMODORE STOCKTON

ON THE

SLAVERY QUESTION.

NEW YORK:
S. W. BENEDICT, PRINTER, 16 SPRUCE STREET.
1850.

MR. WEBSTER TO COMMODORE STOCKTON.

WASHINGTON, March 22, 1850.

MY DEAR SIR :—

I send to you, as an old friend, a copy of my late speech in the Senate. It relates to a subject quite interesting to the country, as connected with the question of proper governments for those new territories which you had an important agency in bringing under the power of the United States.

I would hardly ask your opinion of the general sentiments of the speech, although I know you are a very competent judge ; but that, being out of the strife of politics, your judgment is not likely to be biassed, and that you have as great a stake as any man in the preservation of the Union, and the maintenance of the Government on its true principles.

I am, dear sir,

With great respect, yours,

DANIEL WEBSTER.

COMMODORE STOCKTON.

REPLY OF COMMODORE STOCKTON.

PRINCETON, March 25.

DEAR SIR :—

I thank you for your letter and a copy of the recent speech delivered by you in the Senate of the United States.

I need say nothing in commendation of your course, which has been so generally approved, and will proceed (without referring to any difference of opinion that may seem to exist between us on the subject), to communicate to you my candid and long-cherished opinions on the subject of slavery as it exists in the United States, and the duty of the Government and the people in connection with it.

In view of a national crisis in the affairs of Great Britain, one of her eminent statesmen once said : "In order to be prepared for the trials of these times, we should be possessed of a prompt facility of adverting in all our doubts to some grand and comprehensive truth. In a deep and strong soil must that tree fix its roots, the height of which is to reach to heaven, and the sight of it to the ends of the earth."

A great crisis presents itself in the path of the Republic. Interests of incalculable consequence are involved in it—to you, to myself, to every citizen—consequences not limited to our times, but extending onward to all future generations ; and, if there is anything in the hopes that have been cherished of the universally progressive principles of liberty, to the world for ages to come, "There are times, (says another eminent person,) when the assertion of great principles is the best service a man can render society," and this is such a time. We are all called upon to pause at the present crisis, and consider well what are the demands of duty. It is no time to palter about party distinctions or sectional differences; now, if ever, it becomes us to feel that we are Americans, *only Americans*. It is no time to calculate questions of personal popularity; that sacrifice which any citizen may make is as nothing, if it contributes to save his country. A Jerseyman myself, born on one of those proud battle-fields where American liberty was purchased; bearing a life devoted to the service of the Union—I can withhold nothing from the cause of that Union with which I solemnly believe liberty is herself identified, "one and inseparable."

It appears to me that the polar truth to which the view of our fellow-citizens should be directed in the present emergency, is this—That God works in the affairs of nations, and shapes them to His purposes; and that to ascertain His will we must study in the school of His Providences, and take counsel from the observation of His ways to regulate our own. The destinies of men and of nations are in the bosom of the Most High. He lives in the history of the past; He will live in the history of the future; and he who has most deeply reflected upon the records of the past, has most clearly seen that the great characteristics which have marked the progress of every nation, in every age, have eventually resulted in the accomplishment of some grand design in which the hand of Providence, though for a time obscured by shadows, has been at last clearly and distinctly seen.

Of this our own history furnishes a luminous example. The preparation for the erection of the great temple of civil and religious liberty we now inhabit, began in the discoveries and convulsions of the 15th century. The materials for it were found in men schooled by providential trials, and disciplined to the work they were to commence; and it is as rational to suppose the world was the production of chance, as to suppose that the combination of events which led them to this continent, which cherished and protected their infant colonies, which brought about the Revolution and its results, and has made us what we are, was the work of chance; it is this which inspires me with hope, that He who founded the Republic will save it—that He has great purposes to accomplish yet, and that they will be unfolded through successive years for ages to come, in perfecting the institutions of a rational freedom here, and in extending them to all other continents.

Though men were the instruments, the American Revolution was the work of an unseen Power—the actors in it themselves looked back with astonishment at the course they had taken, and the results that had been accomplished. The greater the event, the more clearly has the hand of Providence always been seen in it—the greater the hero, the more heartfelt always has been his acknowledgment that a superior destiny controlled his actions. The American Constitution is the result of a fearful struggle. Its full price was by no means the sufferings undergone in the conflict. The series of events by which it was accomplished, we are now able to trace distinctly back, through the privations and trials of the early colonists, to the days when popular freedom first began the contest with arbitrary power in the civil wars of England—and its pathway is everywhere marked with patient endurance and costly sacrifice.

Things permanently good are of slow growth—the offspring of hardship, they are made strong through suffering. So universal is this law, that the most hasty minds have a secret misgiving of the efficacy of hasty products; and we would as soon expect undisciplined troops to be equal to the hardships and perils of a dangerous campaign, as that an undisciplined community could triumph in that fiercest of all warfares, the warfare which marks everywhere the pathway to national existence, greatness and virtue.

More than two centuries have passed since the events which were to result in founding the Republic were put in motion; and who does not perceive, both in our colonial and constitutional history, that the process by which we have, within a comparatively few years, come to the full achievement of a distinctive nationality, has been one mainly of forbearance and self-denial? Nor have we been the only sufferers. When our ancestors came to this country, they found it in the possession of another race. That race has had their day. A great continent, fitted by nature for large developments in the progress of humanity, had been for centuries committed to their keeping, and they had proved faithless to their trust. It was manifest from the commencement of the struggles, that one of the two races must give way to the other, and no one doubts the beneficence of that Providence which decided for the Anglo-Saxon race. Yet how touching is the story of the red man's wrongs! We commiserate his sufferings, while we clearly see that the degree by which his race wastes away before the advancing footsteps of civilization, is the fiat of Infinite Wisdom.

The same all-pervading Providence has brought us in contact with still another race—the *African;* but under widely different circumstances. Out of this circumstance, and the events connected with it, the crisis we are now considering has grown. Three millions of that race, scattered through fifteen of the States of the Union, are in the condition of servitude. Individuals in the non-slaveholding States have not only been long in the habit of denouncing the holding of slaves as a sin, as, indeed, among the worst of crimes, but have insisted on immediate and unconditional abolition—have carried on the work of agitation—have encouraged slaves to desert their masters—have protected fugitive slaves from pursuit and reclamation, and have even gone so far as to declare that it was cause for separating from the South altogether.

The general Government has been agitated; compromise after compromise has been made, and proved, as was to be expected, only the means of postponing, rather than of settling the question; until at last things have reached a condition that real danger to the Union seems to be apprehended by the wisest men of both sections of the country. It is time for men now to speak out, calmly but fearlessly. Whatever has been wrong should be made right, and the question settled now and forever. We should not meanly shrink from our just responsibilities and put them upon our children.

Now, in reference to the relation of master and slave, it is proper we should bear in mind that African slavery was introduced into this country by *no act of ours.* For its introduction the American people are in no just sense responsible. Its introduction here was the act of Great Britain, while we were her colonies. She engrafted this system into our communities at a time when these communities (then in their infancy) were unable to make any effectual resistance. Our ancestors, at the time, and through all the process by which it was accomplished, remonstrated and protested against it; but their remonstrances and protests were unheeded. Its introduction was considered by the early colonists an evil—a measure of oppression to them as well as to the slave—but they were as powerless to resist it as the slave himself.

So far as we are concerned, this circumstance in our condition is Providential. If we would presume to scrutinize and judge the ways of Providence, we are driven back to first principles. God rules in the affairs of nations and of men as an absolute sovereign, and shapes all human events to his great purposes. The purposes He designed to accomplish in all this, may be involved in comparative darkness now; but if it shall appear hereafter *that this was the means by which in the lapse of centuries, He accomplished the redemption of Africa herself*, who will say that the means He chose were inconsistent with his wisdom or his goodness?

This fact, then, is undisputed, that when the battles of the Revolution had been fought—when the North and the South had passed shoulder to shoulder through that long and bloody and self-sacrificing struggle, and the independence of their country was achieved, the institution of slavery, planted by other hands in our midst, existed. A very large number of our citizens, both in the North and South, were slaveholders. Property is the creature of the law, and slaves had been made property by law—been so held for ages. What was to be done? The general welfare—the preservation of all that had been gained—the law of self-defence, required that a Government should be established, and that this Government should embrace and combine in one indissoluble union, all the liberated colonies. If that had not been accomplished, all would have been shipwrecked together.

The men of the Revolution saw this plainly. They were men equal to the crisis. They considered the question as a whole. They sacrificed on the altar of concession their different views and interests as to particulars, that they might reach harmoniously the grand result. The articles of confederation, and subsequently the constitution, were the results of compromise—and whatever politicians may say—the spirit—the intent—the fair construction of that compromise is, *that the institution of slavery belongs exclusively to the States, as a matter of State regulation, and that the general government has nothing to do with it.*

No power over it was delegated by the Constitution to the general Government (except as to the importation of Slaves into the States,) nor was any such power prohibited by it to the States. It was expressly provided that persons held to service or labor in one State under the laws thereof, escaping into another, should not be discharged from such service or labor, but should be delivered up on claim of the party to whom such service or labor might be due ; and by an amendment to the Constitution, adopted in 1791, it was provided that the powers not delegated to the United States by the Constitution, nor prohibited by it to the States, are reserved to the States respectively or to the people. Such is the Constitution—such the compromise upon which it was formed—such the imperative necessity of that compromise : and even if that compromise and that Constitution were the result of a *mistake*, it is binding now, and as long as it shall remain unaltered, on every law-abiding man.

If the *toleration* of slavery—if the permission for its existence in any part of the Union was a great national *crime*—when and by whom was that crime committed? At the formation of the government, at the adoption of the Constitution, and by the Washingtons, the Roger Shermans, the Hamiltons, the Madisons, the Franklins, the Pinkneys of the land—by such men as Livingston and Paterson, Brearly and Dayton of my own native State, approved and sanctioned with unparalleled unanimity by the North and South. Under its auspices I need not say with what giant strides the republic has advanced to greatness and prosperity, nor that Heaven has smiled propitiously upon our common heritage.

Now, the question which has come up with such a threatening aspect before the country, is in my judgment one of *morals* not of politics—questions always the most difficult and dangerous to deal with—because they do not lie in notions of expediency, but in matters of conscience. They are always liable to run into fanaticism, and are always mingled with questions of religious faith and moral obligation. The question is one of morals, and as such it is to be settled, if settled permanently at all. Out of this aspect of the case have sprung, as incidents, all the questions that have heretofore been and are now the subjects of discussion. The convention of '87, the Missouri compromise, the contested question of abolition petitions in Congress, the agitations in the North, the recriminations of the South, the difficulties about fugitive slaves, and latterly, the California question and the Wilmot Proviso, are all but branches of one fruitful tree—the question as to the moral character of slavery as it exists in the States, and the moral duty consequent upon that character. In reference to those phases or incidents of this question, which involve the action of the government, they never would have been unsettled, or at any rate never would have come up in their present embarrassing forms, if the general government had adhered, as it ought in my opinion to have adhered, from the beginning, to a strict construction of the Constitution. The framers of this instrument meant to exclude, and by the language of the instrument did exclude the national government from all action upon the subject.

They granted no such power, they expressly excluded all powers not granted. Whenever the doctrine of inferential powers—that latitudinarian doctrine—comes fully to be insisted on and adopted, the Constitution will become itself a thing of wax, to be moulded by the ever-changing opinions of men, into whatever shape those opinions happen to take—the majority will become supreme—its will, the Constitution, and everything conservative, will be liable to be broken down. Suppose a measure oppressive—ruinous to one portion of the Union, is adopted by a mere constitutional majority, and in constitutional form—it is said the party complaining and denying its constitutionality, has an appeal to the Supreme Court. But to argue that that is always to be regarded as a place of absolute security, is to argue that it is infallible. It undergoes the process of change by death; the new incumbents are apt to partake of the views of the Constitution held by a majority of the government, and the Court to become itself the advocate of those views. Beyond this are the rocks, the breakers of revolution; the dernier resort of an oppressed people. The Constitution itself was originally in tended to be the cable and anchor of the Union and all its parts—and nothing, you may rely upon it, but the doctrine of a strict construction can ever preserve it what it was intended to be.

Upon the question of domestic slavery in the States and in the territories, non-intervention is the true principle. There the letter of the Constitution placed it, and there it should be left. The law of nature, fixing the bounds of the institution by the unalterable constitution of the colored race; the temperature of the climate and nature of the soil, and the will of the people acting through the State Legislatures upon their several States, are the true and legitimate regulators; and all interference, except moral suasion, the power of argument, the free expression of opinion, ought to be excluded

I now come to the main question—the question which lies back of all the others. 1st. Is domestic slavery a sin, or an unmitigated evil? and 2d—What is the duty of the people of the non-slaveholding States, respecting it? These questions go to the root of the whole difficulty.

1st. Is domestic slavery a sin, or an unmitigated evil? In order to arrive at an intelligent conclusion respecting the right or the wrong of any complex scheme or any existing institution, we must be careful not to array our feelings against our reason; nor ought we to allow our displeasure at particular cases of excess to interfere with a fair and deliberate consideration of the general working and tendency of the system as a whole. It belongs to this question to consider, first—the condition of the colored man as it would have been had he been left in Africa. 2d. The circumstances under which we find him here. 3d. The necessity, if such there be, of his present continuance in the condition in which we find him. 4th. The ultimate tendency of what may seem to be a Providential arrangement of this state of things.

1st. Of all the races of men with which history and travel have acquainted us, there is none so sunk beyond all hope of self-restoration as the African, on his wide continent. In ignorance so utter, that he is elevated little above the brute; in superstition so gross, that it drags him even lower than the brute; without a thought of liberty, he is the sport of tyranny in its lowest, meanest, and most cruel forms; he has nothing he can call his own; he has no idea of God, of justice, of moral obligation, of the rights of persons or property. In a word, "Africa has long forgotten God and God has abandoned Africa" —but not, I trust, *forever*. From such a land and such a condition—sold, bartered away by his countrymen—the slave was brought to these shores while we were colonists, and subject to British law. Here he is in a civilized and Christian country; he has more opportunities of enlightenment than he would have had in Africa; he is, as a general rule, treated with kindness; he is protected from want in sickness and old age; and is, on the whole, better off, safer, happier, than he would have been in his native country.

2d. But in the second place, with the moral character of the act bringing the slave to this country, we have now nothing to do. We find him here—the thing is done. So far as the slave trade is concerned, we have acted on that, and abolished it. Slavery was introduced in other times and under other auspices. It existed when the government was established; an institution which could not be got rid of—which had of necessity to be tolerated. Slaves had been made property in the Colonies by British law. The Government found it an existing institution, and the Constitution left it so—of necessity, imperative and uncontrollable—to be enacted on exclusively by the States; subject to the moulding and changing and controlling opinions and consciences of those concerned. These have not been inactive. In many of the States the institution has been abolished; in others, meliorated; in all, it is a question for opinion and conscience to act upon. As the General Government has no power to abolish it, so it has no power to prevent any State from abolishing it.

3d. In the third place, every considerate man sees, that in the present condition of things, slavery cannot be immediately and absolutely abolished. We must reason about things as they are—not as we might wish them to be. The slave is property; he became so by a law of our common ancestors; he was left in that condition by the law of our common fathers who founded the Republic. The burden of this purchase should be borne in all justice, equally by our citizens, and we are not ready to pay the price. But if we were ready, he is not in a condition to take care of himself. He has not the culture, the training, the experience, necessary to self-dependence. And where is he to go? No reflecting man is prepared to say he is willing to have three millions of slaves turned loose in the States, to fill the prisons and poor-houses and alms-houses of the country, or to live by plunder on the community. What, too, is to be his lot for the future in such a case? Is he to live in our midst as a marked and degraded being, through all time, or are we prepared to place him on an equality with us, civilly and socially. Are we ready for amalgamation?

There seems under those circumstances to be a necessity for his continuance at present in the condition in which he is placed.

In the fourth place, the hand of Providence seems to be clearly pointing out an ultimate design in all this arrangement of things. Yonder is Africa, with her one hundred and fifty millions of miserable, degraded, ignorant, lawless, superstitious idolaters. Whoever has stood upon her sands, has stood upon a continent that has geographical and physical peculiarities which belong to no other of the great divisions of the globe. The latter appear, upon the face of them, to have been adapted to draw out the energies of the natives in their inequalities of temperature, soil, and surface, inviting the ingenuity and enterprise of man to overcome them, and in the varieties of their products tempting the interchanges of commerce; thus affording ample encouragement to the progress of civil and social improvement. But Africa is still, as of old, a land of silence and of mystery. Like the interminable dreariness of her own deserts, her moral wastes of mind lie waiting for the approach of influences from abroad. No savage people have ever advanced to a civilized state without intercommunication with others. All the continents of the world have, in their turn, been occupied and civilized by means of colonies; but in no one of them did it appear so inevitably necessary, from a previous examination of circumstances, as in that of Africa. It is plain to the very eye, that Africa is a land to which civilization *must be brought*. The attempt has been made over and over again by devoted missionaries and others to penetrate that land, and seek to impart the blessings of civilization and Christianity to her savage hordes. But the labor has been spent in vain. The white man cannot live in Africa. The annals of the Moravians, of Cape Colony, of Sierra Leone, of Liberia, contain the records of the sacrifice of some of the best men that have lived to grace the pages of any people's history, in the vain attempt to accomplish something for her redemption through the instrumentality of white men. *Who, then, is to do this work?*

Let now any calm, reflecting spectator of the present state of the world be asked to look at Africa, and then, from among the nations point out the people best calculated to do this work—and when his eye falls upon the descendants of the sons of that continent now in America, will he not say, *These are the people appointed for that work?*

The ways of God are mysterious. So Joseph was sold a slave into Egypt; so his father and his brethren were driven thither by providential circumstances; so their generations remained as slaves in Egypt for four centuries and a half; and when the appointed time had come, in His own appointed way, the Ruler of nations led them to the accomplishment of His great purposes. And it is not to be forgotten, that it was not the act of holding this people in bondage for so many years, that Pharaoh and the Egyptians were punished; but their crime was this: that when the Divine Being had prepared all things for the event he proposed to accomplish, and demanded, by an accredited ambassador, that they should be allowed to depart, "they would not let the people go."

The great progenitor of the Israelites was a slaveholder; the Israelites, after their emancipation, became slaveholders. Nothing is clearer than that under the Mosaic dispensation, slavery was lawful; the institution was recognized and regulated by the law of Moses; and the founder of Christianity and his disciples (though Judea and all the provinces of the Roman empire were in their times full of slaves, and slaves subjected to the most rigid laws), never forbade or even denounced the relation as sinful, or exhorted masters to liberate their slaves; but enjoined on masters the principles of humanity and justice, and on slaves obedience and contentment; and those notions of morality may well be questioned, which in our days disallow what Christ and his apostles did not disallow."

Such an Exodus as that of the Jews from Egypt may not be

within the purpose of the Deity in relation to the children of Africa now in this country, or their descendants. But has He no purpose in all this arrangement that has been going on, in the gathering of a vast family of these people here, in their condition of servitude, endurance, discipline—in the difficulties with which their emancipation is surrounded—in the natural impossibility that the whites ever will or can consent to raise them to a condition of equality? No purpose in casting their lot in a country so free for the interchange of opinion, and where opinion is so enlightened and progressive, and there is so much benevolence and Christian enterprise? Has he not a purpose in all this, to accomplish (in some way of his own, through this instrumentality) the regeneration of the millions of benighted Africa? The germs of Colonies are already planted there, as the fruits of this system of servitude. But the free African among us clings to this country still, under all his disabilities, regardless of the claims of the land of his fathers upon him; and may not *slavery and the necessity of migration as the condition* of his release, be the appointed instrument to produce compliance? The colonies we have settled in Africa would, ere this day, have become a Republic of power, had the free negroes of the North been willing to become citizens of it. But, like the Israelities of old, who would but for the Divine interposition, have sacrificed their liberators in the wilderness, and returned into Egypt, these liberated descendants of Africa cannot be persuaded to look toward the land of their fathers. The millions of their colored bondmen *there* awaken no sympathy in their hearts. Their fixed and resoluted purpose appears to be to remain among the whites, and force themselves by progressive steps into a civil and social equality with them; and it is chiefly with a view to strengthen themselves in these particular views and aspirations, that they band together under the abolition flag, and fill our cities with threats of vengeance against the white race, if they shall dare to execute the laws in relation to fugitive slaves.

Now, when we come to reflect calmly and candidly upon all these circumstances, in connection with the question—is domestic slavery, as it exists at the South, *a sin?* it seems to me that question must be answered in the *negative*. The relation of master and slave may be, and doubtless is, sometimes the occasion of cruelty and injustice. But this is also true of the relation of husband and wife, parent and child, master and apprentice, and of employer and employed in our system of labor. But the abuses of a system or relation form no sound argument against the system or relation itself. I am no apologist for abuse. I am as ready as any man to denounce cruelty, unnatural separations, a disregard of the domestic relations, or a deprivation of the means of moral and religious culture to the slave, under our system of slavery, as a crime. But the correction of these belongs to the duties of the State Governments. We, in New Jersey, have no more right to interfere with South Carolina, than she with us, in such matters—nor in fact have we in New Jersey any more right to interfere with the slaves of South Carolina or Georgia, than we have with the slaves of Russia or Austria. Each Southern State being, in respect to this question, as absolutely sovereign as are Russia and Austria. We are to reason about the institution of Slavery as we reason about every other human institution, from its proper, humane, conscientious and lawful *use*, when both parties discharge their mutual obligations.

Having established, as I think, that domestic Slavery, as it exists in the Southern States, is not in itself sinful or an unmitigated evil, this subject is relieved from its greatest embarrassment, and now I proceed to consider: *What is the duty of the people of non-Slave-holding States respecting Slavery*?

Shall we attempt forcibly to break down this institution of Slavery? To make the attempt is:

First. To violate the Constitution and its compromises. I care not whether under color of inferential instruction—assuming the Constitution to imply the power of interference—(which, by the way, I unconditionally deny)—or acting regardless of it. In either case, it is at best, the appeal to the mere majority power, acting upon and forcing the minority.

Second. It is to attempt the liberation of the slave, and fail. For by the effort the most we can do is to drive the South with its slaves out of the Union without liberating a single slave; and,

Third. It is to *compel a dissolution of the Union*. Have the people considered the consequences implied in this branch of the alternative? Suppose, after all, that in opposition to the plain teachings of the Bible, and the judgment of God's holiest men, they still hold that slavery is in itself *sinful, and the owners of slaves are men stealers, robbers and pirates*, then, indeed, this question assumes a more serious aspect, and Mr. Calhoun may no longer be denounced as either unpatriotic or extravagant in calling for an amendment of the Constitution, or any other means that will secure his constituents from imminent peril, and his posterity from the calamities of civil war. But—

Is there not, in this view, a crime of deeper and redder dye, in marching over a desecrated Bible and a broken compact to shed oceans of fraternal blood? Is it lawful, on their own principles, to do evil that good may come—even if good could by it be accomplished? If they succeed in driving the South to a secession, they inevitably kindle the fire of a conflagration which will burn over this whole Republic, until it reduces to ashes the structure which Providence has for centuries been preparing and rearing up on this continent; and, in the conflagration, their own homes and hopes will be mingled with the sacrifice.

"One great principle," says Dr. Channing, "which we should lay down as immovably true, is, that if a good work cannot be carried on by the calm, self-controlled, benevolent spirit of Christianity, then the time for doing it has not come. *God asks not the aid of our vices.* He can overrule them for good, but they are not the chosen instruments of human happiness." But if we would adopt, as I sincerely do, the other alternative—that with the institution of slavery as its exists in the South, we have nothing to do—that we are not only prohibited by the Constitution from meddling with it, but that it is a question of conscience to be settled by Southern men for themselves—a question upon which good men may differ, and must be left to differ if they will, whether in the North or South—a new train of thoughts, a new field of benevolent and Christian enterprise opens before us. Going back to the great truth from which we started, and regarding all the circumstances of the present state of things as a part of the design of Providence to accomplish a great result for Africa, there is a work and a great work for us to do. Let the great heart of Christian benevolence in the North and the South unite in selecting from this vast African family, this nursery planted and growing on our shores, the proper subjects to be sent upon the mission of redemption to the land of their ancestors, until the last slave shall have departed, and Africa's long night shall have been dispelled by the sun of freedom and civilization. The philanthropist will find here enough to do to satisfy the largest benevolence—in acts, in personal sacrifices, in contributions to the cause of humanity, without the violation of personal or legal rights—doing *good* that *good* may come.

Let the general government then retrace its steps—and instead of provisos and compromise lines, and agreements to keep up the balance of power—fall back upon the literal construction of the Constitution—adopt the principle of *total non-intervention*, now and forever—leaving the laws of nature, and the voice of public opinion to adjust the limits of the institution, free, uncontrolled, and uninfluenced by the action of Congress, and all will be safe. The gordian knot will be dissolved—not cut—and the ark of the covenant, with its sacred deposit, be borne on safely to its destination.

The measures, in short, which I would propose, are—

1st. A declarative act in such form as may be deemed proper, that the Constitution gives no power to the general Government to act on the subject of domestic slavery, either with respect to its existence in the States, the Territories or the District of Columbia.

2d. The most efficient act that can be framed to enforce the provisions of the Constitution in relation to fugitive slaves.

3d. That California, in consideration of the peculiar circumstances of her case, be admitted without the approval or disapproval of that part of her constitution which relates to slavery.

I believe these three positions, carried out, would settle the question forever. They involve no concessions—no compromise—they are no temporary expedient. They put the solution of the difficulty on the eternal principles of right—the law of the Constitution.

I think the great majority of the North and South are prepared to place it there, and having placed it there, to stand by and maintain the Union at all hazards.

I feel that I have already trespassed too long on your patience. But it is a subject of vast importance, and I cannot close this letter without a few general remarks in reference to the foregoing views.

At such a time all good men will forbear, exchange opinions, and reason in the spirit of conciliation.

Conscientious differences of opinion among men will always exist in relation to moral questions.

Some conscientious men believe slavery to be a sin—other conscientious men believe that the law of property which enables one man to hold what they insist is the common gift of the Creator to his creatures, is sin. Again, still, other conscientious men hold that to take a glass of wine is sin, and so on through an endless variety of subjects.

If these conscientious opinions, or any of them, pervade the majority, are all who do not hold them to be driven with fire and sword out of the Union, or compelled to yield their opinions, equally conscientious, to the majority? These notions are inconsistent with a wise moderation; they come from an abuse of reason in the first place, and a proposed abuse of power in the second.

Such arguments are always drawn principally from the *excesses* of a system, rather than from the system itself, and there lies the error; it is the error of *fanaticism* which always puts in the plea of conscience, whether it burns the supposed heretic at the stake, or hunts down witchcraft, or impales the Nestorian, or fans the flame of civil war.

Instead of railing with infuriated declamation against a system, because of its excesses, which are incident to every human institution, we should calmly and dispassionately seek to extract the truth from the general rule rather than from its exceptions. The system of slavery, like every human system, has its excesses, its exceptions from the general rule. But it is quite probable that there may exist in the one, as in the other, an absolute law, which is working out a beneficent result. If a man wishes to fall under the delusion of a universal fanaticism, it is only necessary that he adopt the method of looking at the special attendants of every system, to the exclusion of the general law which regulates them, and the work is done; while he is intent with some accident of the train, the train itself has long since passed on, leaving him to grow more and more inflated with conceit, indignation, unholy zeal and misanthropic railing; all the natural results of so narrow minded a procedure. Let every man run off with particular features out of the general complexion of any subject or thought, and gaze at those features long enough and absorbingly enough, and the best thing within the range of human experience, will become to him a bugbear. The individual, however, who neglects the "great law of compensation" in judging of human affairs, has only to apply the same method of judging to himself—and passing by his redeeming qualities, and looking only at his own excesses and defects, he will find in himself, if he is honest in the search, enough to satiate his appetite for condemnation and hate. It is far easier to condemn than to judge correctly—far easier to get into a passion about a subject than to get a comprehension of it.

The idea that out of the institution of domestic slavery in this country is to spring the regeneration of Africa, derives, it seems to me, great force from the recurrence to past history.

We invariably find that in the dispensation of Providence, nations which have been called to act an important part in the work of human progress, have been led through a long previous discipline of trial; the restraints and endurance of youth have preceded the power and efficiency of manhood. Primary subjection is the law of stable growth, and seems an indispensable condition of the advancement of our race.

We have only to look back through a few centuries to find the evidences of this in the annals of our race. Our ancestors were for centuries a down-trodden, enslaved and toiling people. The Anglo-Saxon race have become what they are, by a long training in the school of patient endurance; in the case of England, under oppressive servitude to the Roman and the Norman; in the case of America, under the oppression of our mother country and the trying discipline of Colonial suffering. In the life of a nation, hundreds of years may be as a day in the life of an individual. It is often necessary for many generations to pass, before a new influence can be made to affect the mass. If all were willing, the work of national preparation might be more rapid; but thousands are to be made willing—and by the Providential adaptation of the means to the end.

It is conceded, on all hands, that the probation of the African people, now in bondage on our shores, is to come to an end.

That while there is an interchange of benefits between the parties, there is at the same time a community of evil, which renders it better, both for the whites and the blacks, that it should come to an end.

When shall that time be, is the great question before the American people.

In seeking an answer to this question, we may be sure there is some safer ground on which to take our stand, than that of political chicane, of fanatical prejudice, or of any merely temporary or prudential expediency.

If slavery is to be abolished now, then it is to be done in a moment. That is to say, at one stroke a community of three millions of people, habituated to a certain way of life, are to be thrown into new circumstances—a thing plainly preposterous, because no kind of society changes its customs suddenly and succeeds in doing well. Great changes in society must come in with previous preparation, or they come in to little purpose. Seven years sufficed to fight the battles of the revolution, but many more were spent in preparation for that event, and many more will be required to perfect its results. If Providence rules in the affairs of nations, the existence of slavery has some prospective purpose, only to be accomplished by prior preparation for it.

Let us not be impatient or presumptuous. These African people are passing to their destiny along the same path which has been trod by other nations, through a mixture of hardship, of endurance, but in a land of light, and amid a civilized society. They are preparaing to accomplish a work for their native continent, which no other people in the world can accomplish. Their plain mission is, ultimately to carry the gifts of society, of religion, of government, to the last remaining continent of the earth—where these blessings are totally unknown. Their work is a great one, as it would seem to be connected essentially with the final and universal triumph of civilization and Christianity, in the world. It is our duty to follow, not to attempt to lead in the ways and purposes of Providence. We are to move forward when the pillar of fire and cloud moves forward; and to rest when it rests.

Doubtless there is a time for action ; but it is characteristic of all great changes that they make known their own seasons. That time, in the present instance, has not yet come—for the manifest reason that the way is not yet open for it. When the time shall come, the way will come with it, the preparations for it be complete. The North settled this question, easily, quietly. Surely it is no great stretch of charity for us to suppose that in due time the same thing will be accomplished in the South. We of the North have given no peculiar evidence of superior goodness that we should suppose the South not to be possessed of as much justice, charity, and good sense as ourselves.

I firmly believe that the hour for the complete enfranchisement of the Southern Slave, will be the hour of the complete preparation for the work of African redemption and civilization—and that hour will make itself known *in the removal of all obstacles here and there;* in the preparation of the workmen and the work ; and I earnestly hope that guided by happier influences than seem now to pervade the country, the pulpit, the press, the people of the North and the South, may give their thoughts and efforts to this subject in the spirit of Him, whose mission to our earth was heralded by the proclamation of peace and good will.

With great regard, yours,

R. F. STOCKTON.

www.ingramcontent.com/pod-product-compliance
Lightning Source LLC
LaVergne TN
LVHW011144110826
845150LV00008B/2501

* 9 7 8 1 4 1 8 1 9 2 0 3 7 *